Rookie
Read-About®
Health

I Need Stitches

by Lisa M. Herrington

Content Consultant
Catherine A. Dennis, N.P.

Reading Consultant
Jeanne M. Clidas, Ph.D.
Reading Specialist

Children's Press®
An Imprint of Scholastic Inc.
New York Toronto London Auckland Sydney
Mexico City New Delhi Hong Kong
Danbury, Connecticut

Library of Congress Cataloging-in-Publication Data
Herrington, Lisa M.
 I need stitches/by Lisa M. Herrington.
      pages cm. — (Rookie read-about health)
Summary: "Introduces the reader to what stitches are, why they might need them,
and how to care for them"— Provided by publisher.
Audience: Ages 3-6
Includes bibliographical references and index.
   ISBN 978-0-531-21039-0 (library binding: alk. paper) — ISBN 978-0-531-21114-4
(pbk.: alk. paper) —
ISBN 0-531-21114-2 (pbk.: alk. paper)
1. Sutures—Juvenile literature. 2. Wound healing—Juvenile literature. I. Title. II. Series:
Rookie read-about health.

 RD73.S8H47 2015
 617.1'3—dc23   2014035909

Produced by Spooky Cheetah Press
Design by Keith Plechaty

© 2015 by Scholastic Inc.

All rights reserved. Published in 2015 by Children's Press, an imprint of Scholastic Inc.

Printed in China 62

SCHOLASTIC, CHILDREN'S PRESS, ROOKIE READ-ABOUT®, and associated logos
are trademarks and/or registered trademarks of Scholastic Inc.

1 2 3 4 5 6 7 8 9 10 R 24 23 22 21 20 19 18 17 16 15

Photographs ©: Alamy Images: 29 top left (Israel Talby/Israel images), 29 bottom
(Phovoir), 3 top left, 24, 28 (Vote Photography/VStock); Getty Images: 15 (Rafe
Swan/Cultura Science), cover (Tanya Little); iStockphoto: 27, 31 bottom (DIGIcal),
20, 31 center bottom (Michael Krinke); Media Bakery/C. Lyttle: 8; Shutterstock,
Inc.: 16 (Anukool Manoton), 29 top right (pedalist); Superstock, Inc.: 7 (Cusp), 30
(Minden Pictures); Thinkstock: 4 (anatols), 19 (Comstock), 31 top (Fedor Kondratenko),
3 bottom (Nathan Allred), 31 center top (Nathan Allred), 11 (SergiyN), 23
(Wavebreakmedia Ltd), 3 top right (Zerzaaman).

Table of Contents

When You Need Stitches

Ouch! You fell off your bike.
The cut on your leg is deep.
It will not stop bleeding.
You need **stitches**!

All kids get cuts and scrapes. Stitches are not for small cuts. They are used to help big or deep cuts heal well. Stitches help stop bleeding. They keep a cut from getting **infected**.

Most small cuts bleed for only a short time.

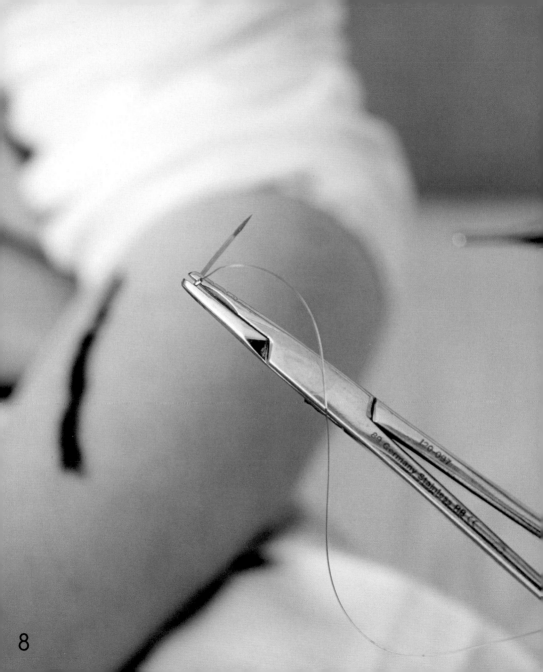

Stitches are pieces of thread
that close a cut in the skin.
A doctor uses stitches to sew the
skin together. Once the skin heals,
the stitches come out.

FAST FACT!

Stitches are usually in place from a few
days to a couple of weeks. The amount
of time depends on the cut and spot.

Your Amazing Skin

Your skin protects your body. It keeps you from getting too hot or too cold. It gives you the sense of touch. When you get a small cut, your skin mends itself if you care for the wound properly.

FAST FACT!

Skin is the body's biggest organ.

Layers of Skin

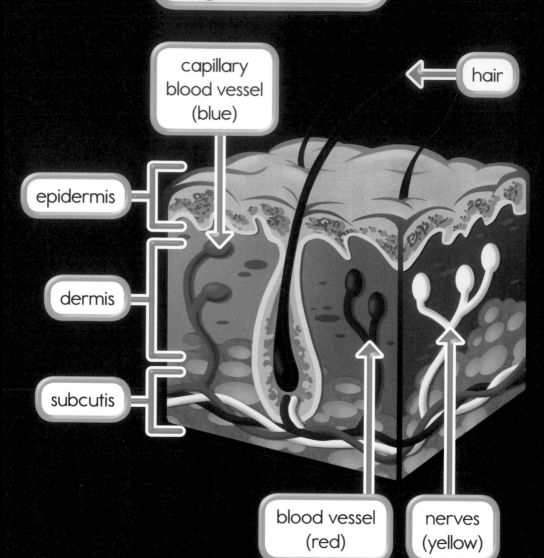

capillary blood vessel (blue)

hair

epidermis

dermis

subcutis

blood vessel (red)

nerves (yellow)

Stitches help a deep cut heal faster. Your skin has three layers. The top layer is called the epidermis (EP-ih-dur-miss). Next is the dermis. It contains blood vessels and nerves that let you feel. The bottom layer of fat is called the subcutis (sub-CUE-tiss). It connects to your bones and muscles.

Getting Stitches

Before working on your cut, the doctor will put a gel on the area to be stitched. That will **numb** your skin. The doctor may also use a small needle to put liquid numbing medicine into your skin. You will not feel much after that.

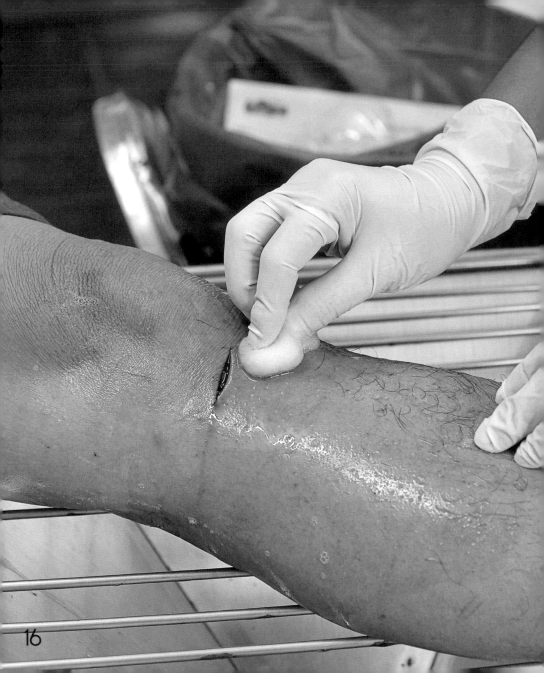

The doctor will clean the cut. Any glass or dirt will be removed. The doctor will put in the stitches. You may feel a tug as the cut is stitched. Then the doctor will put a bandage over the stitches to protect them and keep them clean.

A doctor cleans a cut.

Stitches may also be used to seal the skin after an operation. During an operation, a doctor fixes or removes something inside the body.

FAST FACT!

There are other ways to close big cuts. Special staples or medical glue may be used on some wounds.

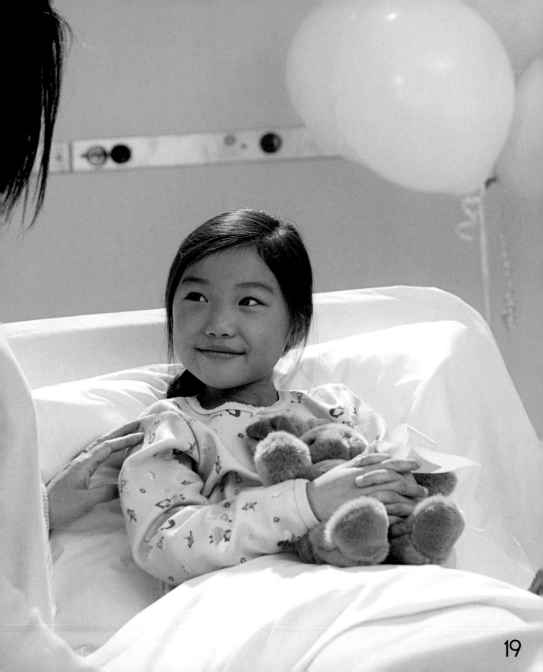

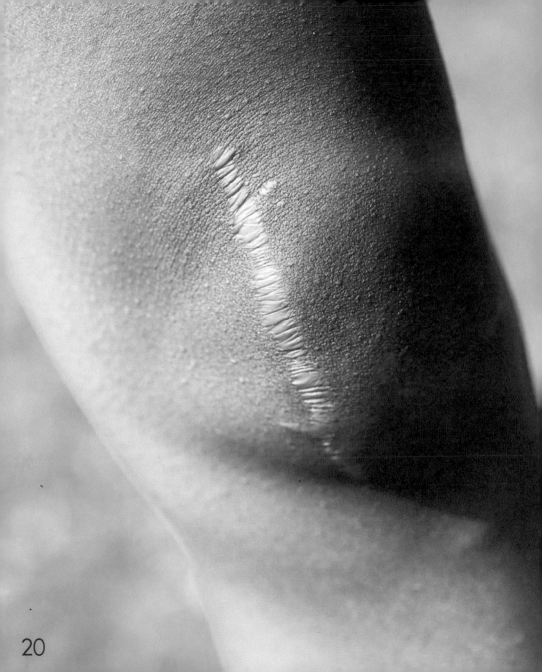

A cut that needs stitches may leave a **scar**. A scar is a mark on your skin that remains after the cut has healed. In time, the scar may fade.

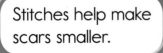

Stitches help make scars smaller.

Caring for Stitches

Taking care of stitches will help the cut heal right. Most stitches should not get wet. You may need to put medicine or bandages on them.

Do not tug or pull on stitches even if they are itchy. You should never try to take out your own stitches.

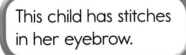
This child has stitches in her eyebrow.

Some stitches come out on their own. The doctor takes out other kinds. The thread is gently pulled out. Before you know it, your skin will be healed!

FAST FACT!

Stitches in the mouth often fall out on their own.

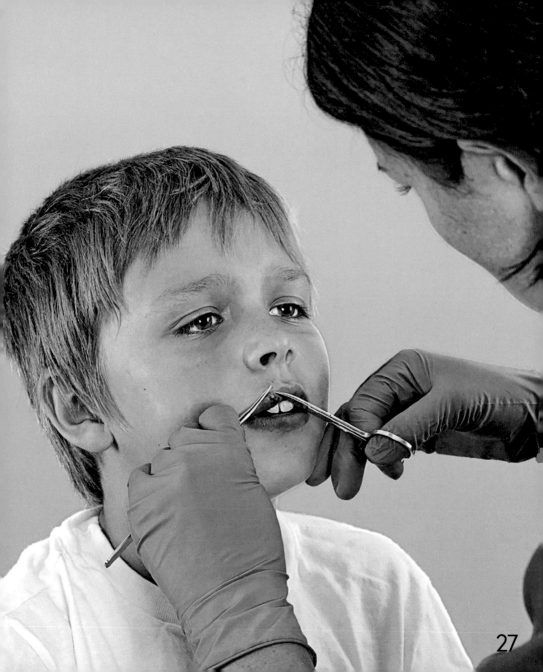

Your Turn

Show What You Know

Take this quiz to show what you know about stitches and your skin.

1. Stitches help deep cuts heal.　　True　False

2. Some types of stitches fall out on their own.　　True　False

3. Scratching stitches is okay.　　True　False

4. A bandage helps keep stitches clean.　　True　False

Answers: 1. True 2. True 3. False: Scratching can damage stitches. 4. True

Stitches Smarts

Look at the photos below. Which one shows the wrong way to treat stitches?

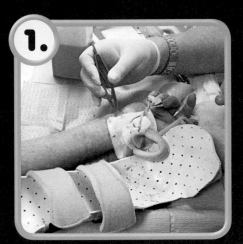

Answer: 2. You should never scratch or pull at your stitches.

Strange but True!

Eewww! Long ago, people used army ants as stitches. These ants have strong jaws. The ants were placed over a cut. They closed their jaws when they bit the skin. The rest of the ant was removed. The jaw was left on as a stitch.

Just for Fun

Q: What did your skin say to your bones?

A: I've got you covered!

Q: What did the cut on the back part of the foot say?

A: Don't worry. I'll heel.

Glossary

infected (in-FEKT-ed): affected by germs that cause disease

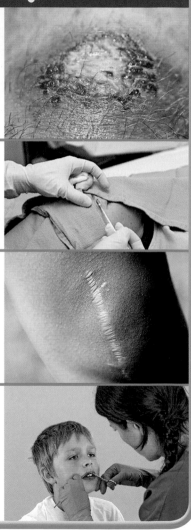

numb (NUHM): cause a lack of feeling or pain

scar (SKAR): mark left on skin from a cut that has healed

stitches (STICH-es): thread used to close a cut in the skin

Index

Facts for Now

Visit this Scholastic Web site for more information on stitches:
www.factsfornow.scholastic.com
Enter the keyword **Stitches**

About the Author

Lisa M. Herrington is the author of many books and articles for kids. She lives in Trumbull, Connecticut, with her husband, Ryan, and daughter, Caroline.